The moon and planets reflect light from the Sun. When light is reflected, it bounces off a surface and then continues zooming forward in a new direction.

(Reflected light is also how you see most things, like mountains, trees, and people!)

Lightning emits light from static electricity in rain clouds. The energy that makes the electricity comes from sunlight heating the Earth and lifting the clouds into the sky. When tiny cloud particles bump into each other, they make sparks! And lots of little sparks add up to big sparks!!

Fire emits light by burning fuel. The fuel—in this case, wood—gets its energy from sunlight when it's a living tree. The energy is then stored in the wood until released by burning.

For you, bright reader, full of light!

And for my two boys,
the light of my life—the Rays of my days!

DIAL BOOKS FOR YOUNG READERS
An imprint of Penguin Random House LLC
1745 Broadway, New York, New York, 10019

First published in the United States of America by Dial Books For Young Readers,
an imprint of Penguin Random House LLC, 2025

Library of Congress Cataloging-in-Publication Data is available.

Manufactured in China • ISBN 9780593857984 • 10 9 8 7 6 5 4 3 2
TOPL

This book was edited by Jessica Dandino Garrison, copyedited and proofread by Regina
Castillo, and designed by Jason Henry and Jennifer Kelly. The production was supervised
by Jayne Ziemba, Nicole Kiser, and Vicki Olsen. Text set in Avenir.

The artwork for this book was painted by Emily Kate Moon using
India ink on paper and Photoshop. Ray is made of light itself—
created with only photons in Photoshop!

Special thanks to all the scientists who learn these facts; to the

RAY

How Light Works

EMILY KATE MOON

DIAL BOOKS FOR YOUNG READERS

Light has been here since the beginning of time.

Let's get things started!

Ray and his friends
come from the stars and
they travel through space.

They are here, there, everywhere!

We keep it lit!

Some of them have been traveling through space for billions of years!

We are space explorers!

Nothing in the universe reaches farther than light.

Ray's journey to Earth starts in the Sun, our closest star.

After bouncing around inside the Sun for years, Ray and his friends zoom out, full of energy!

Wheee!

Weightless, they speed through space, ready to share their energy wherever they land.

I'm traveling light!

Ray and his friends travel straight to Earth
from the Sun.

Here, they energize our
special planet,
full of life!

Oh, lucky us!
Earth!

But before they touch ground,
they need to get through
the atmosphere.

Have you met Puff?

He's air.

Welcome to Earth!

Puff makes sure Ray only brings helpful energy to our planet.

Thank you!

Visible light?

Radio waves?

check!

check!

Phew!

When Ray reaches Earth, he lights up the place!

What a lovely day!

He also *warms* it up!

Ray creates heat when he touches things.

Let's turn up the heat!

Oh goody!

Do you know Drop?

She's water.

Ray heats up Drop so she can float with Puff.

And Ray heats up Puff too, so he can move around and carry Drop.

Heat makes Drop and Puff grow bigger and lighter so they can fly away!

Ray keeps Drop and Puff soaring around the world, bringing rain and fresh air everywhere.

keeping the flow...

So fresh!

All winds and rains are powered by light.

I power the weather!

And after a rainstorm, these pals put on a spectacular light show!

But how does this light show work?

It's not always obvious, but Ray is actually a rainbow in disguise!

Check this out!

When all the colors mix together, they look white.

But when Ray and his friends travel through misty air or a glass prism at just the right angle . . .

they bend,
and bounce,
and fan out to reveal . . .

their true colors!

Catch us if you can!

All color is from light!

When you see anything, you really just see light. Ray zooms around, bounces off things in different ways, and then shows them to your eyes with his colors.

Ray gives color to the world!

I am color!

Everything—from the sky to your skin to the spectrum on this page— gets its color from light.

White light, and all the colors, are the parts of Ray that we can see.
But Ray has invisible energy too!

There's more to me than meets the eye...

higher energy

Gamma Rays

These are the highest-energy waves and they are harmful to life. Luckily, our atmosphere protects us from these waves.

Dr. Ray!

X-rays

These high-energy waves can travel through things and help us see inside.

Ultraviolet Rays

These waves break things down—including our skin! We use sunblock, clothes, and shade to protect ourselves from catching too many of these waves.

Visible

Here's how it works: Ray rides waves as he moves.
Some waves come close together and some come far apart.

The type of wave Ray rides depends on how much energy he has.
And Ray can do different things on each wave.

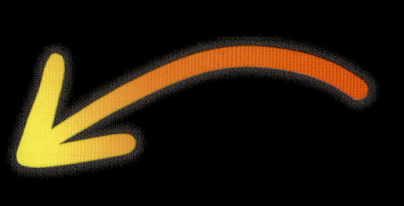

Ray is only visible to our
eyes when he rides these
waves here.

lower   energy

Light Rays   **Infrared Rays**   **Microwaves**   **Radio Waves**

Our skin can feel this light   These low-energy waves
as heat. We use these   shake up water and
waves in ovens, stoves,   make heat. We use this
and fires to cook and bake   light to cook our food in
our food.   microwave ovens.

These very low-
energy waves carry
information to our
radios, cell phones,
and WiFi.

I'm an invisible cook!

Brilliant!

Ray can do so many different things!

And he helps all living things in all sorts of ways.

Hello life!

Ray warms up mammals,
who sunbathe to relax . . .

You're getting sleepy...

and he heats up reptiles and insects,
who sunbathe to get moving.

You're charging up!

Ray helps birds by baking away pests that live in their feathers.

zap!

zap!

And he helps humans and many other animals make vitamin D, which is good for bones.

It's the sunshine vitamin!

But mostly, Ray energizes plants, which helps everybody!

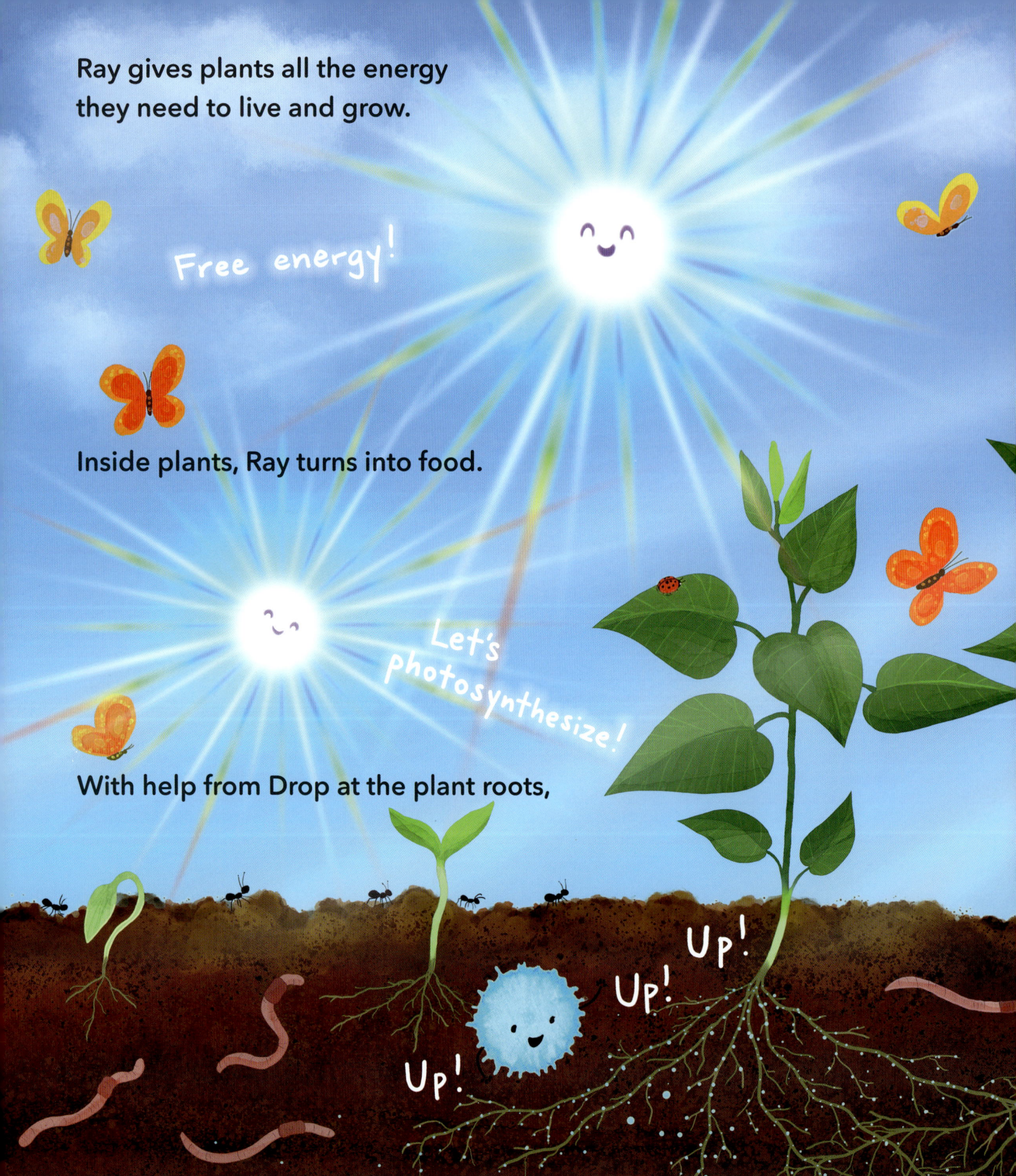

Ray gives plants all the energy they need to live and grow.

Free energy!

Inside plants, Ray turns into food.

Let's photosynthesize!

With help from Drop at the plant roots,

Up!

Up!

Up!

All the energy in food is from light.

I'm the main ingredient!

At the surface of the sea, Ray grows tiny plankton . . .

Hi phytoplankton!

and then he moves
through food chains,
feeding animals
like krill

and fish

and whales . . .

Look at all of you!

Ray and his friends energize plants and plankton that live on light . . .

Light for life!

and then become food for all other earthlings,

even creatures who live in the dark.

They pass through the tiniest living things . . .

Oooh decomposers !

and into the soil.

Down here, they are buried, no longer light, but still energy.

Still got it!

Some of Ray's friends become food for plants,

some escape as heat,

and some stay underground for a long, long time.

Nutrients!

See ya!

Look! Fossils!!

Way down here, stuck in coal and oil, energy can stay in the ground for millions and billions of years.

Wherever they go, Ray and his friends make things happen—
lighting up our world and energizing life!

When Ray reaches you,
how do you use his energy?

You see things in color.

Oh, what fun!

You warm up.

You cook
and eat food.

You grow and change.

SOLAR ENERGY ON EARTH

HEAT AND MOTION:

Sunlight turns into heat when it touches the surface of Earth. Heat expands air and creates wind. The wind pushes huge turbines that turn motion into electricity.

FOOD AND LIFE:

Solar energy is what powers life on Earth. Sunlight turns into sugar inside plants (and phytoplankton!) when they photosynthesize. This captured sunlight is the energy they use to grow. When they grow, plants feed the rest of life on Earth. All of us eat plants—or eat animals that eat plants. This means all life is powered by solar energy!

FOSSIL FUELS:

This solar energy used to be alive! It was captured by living plants and plankton long ago. Solar energy powers life, and has done so for billions of years. When life ends, the bodies of plants and animals decompose into the soil and their remaining energy moves on as heat and nutrients. But, long ago, some plants and plankton didn't decompose—they got stuck under layers of dirt and rock—trapping their remaining solar energy. Humans have relied on digging up this ancient buried sunlight in the form of coal, oil, and natural gas to burn as fuel. Today, we are looking for cleaner ways to use solar energy.